Contents

Don't turn this page!
Think of all the little
things you wear to protect
yourself when you are at
school or playing sport.
See if you recognize any
of them in this book.

Introduction

The things you wear on your body are your costume. You probably have things you like to wear and things you have to wear. Your family probably likes you to wear special clothes for certain occasions. Sometimes what you like to wear and what your family wants you to wear are very different. Have you heard someone say, 'I wouldn't be caught dead in that dress/jacket/hat/shoes'? People can feel very strongly about what they, and others, wear.

▼ 'FUNK INC' poster from funkessentials, designed in 1993

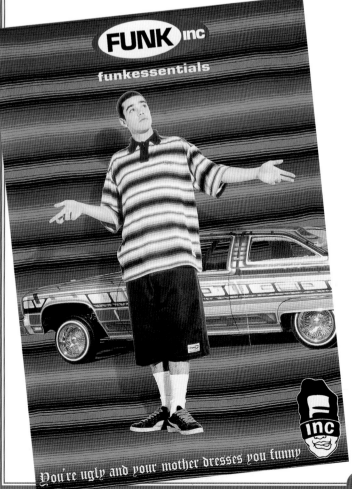

The story of costume is about people's creativity and the ways they like to show it. What people make, wear and care about are examples of this creativity. What people wear says something about them. *Costume* looks at wearing and making clothes across times, places and cultures.

Don't get dressed up to read this book – just dust off your imagination. Start off by imagining yourself without costume.

Too revealing? The strange thing is, the more you cover up with costume, the more you are really saying about yourself.

▶ Transparent plastic figure of a woman. It is full size, and shows the body organs, veins and arteries. It was made in 1954 to teach people about health and hygiene.

Protective clothing

Many animals have an **exoskeleton** – their skeleton acts as a protective shield on the outside of their body. Other animals have a thick coat. Human bodies are soft, with the skeleton under the skin and flesh. It needs protection. Costume made and worn for protection says…

Clothing that is only useful is generally not very pretty, for example, surgical gloves. Interesting fabric, colour or decoration can make even practical clothes more appealing. Practical clothes made for work or sport can be fashionable. Sometimes it depends on how the costume is worn or who wears it.

The costumes in this book are protective and practical. These clothes are mainly concerned with doing the job, not how they look.

'I'm working'

'I'm sporty and fashionable'

'It's raining'

'It's cold'

Armour

Armour protected people against swords, guns and clubs when they fought wars face to face. As weapons changed, armour had to change as well so that it could continue to protect the wearer. With the development of better metalworking techniques, and therefore better swords and arrowheads, armour changed from chainmail, boiled leather and occasional sections of metal to a solid suit of metal. With the invention of firearms, armour became thicker and heavier.

▼ A reproduction of German armour from the 1400s, made in 1890 in England

Japanese armour

Japanese armour was made from metals such as iron, copper, silver and gold; Japanese **lacquer**; leather; and material such as silk or cotton. Beating, heating and folding the iron many times made it very strong. Mixing or heating copper, silver and gold made different colours and patterns.

A samurai warrior

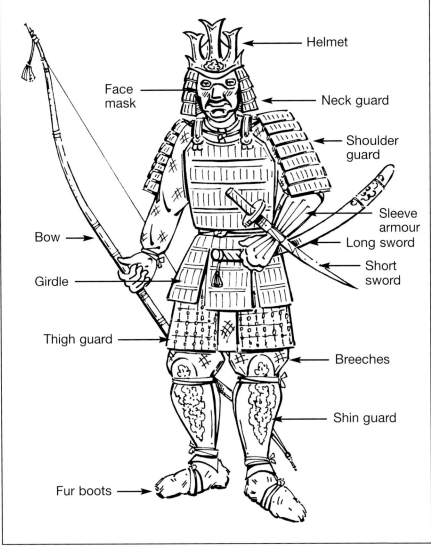

Helmet

Face mask

Neck guard

Shoulder guard

Bow

Sleeve armour

Long sword

Short sword

Girdle

Thigh guard

Breeches

Shin guard

Fur boots

▼ This suit of Japanese armour was made in 1775 for a **samurai** warrior. It was made in the peaceful Edo period of 1600–1868. Although this armour was made for war, it was more likely worn as a ceremonial costume at court.

People with great skill put each piece of armour together. One suit of armour needed many different makers. In the Edo period (1600–1868), certain families made different parts of the armour such as the lacing and the tailoring.

How armour is made today

Mark Jamieson is a full-time professional armourer. Mark started making armour ten years ago as a hobby and has worked as an armourer full time for five years. This is how he makes armour.

◀ A pair of pauldrons for a suit of armour worn in the 1500s

Step 1

Pieces of the **pauldron** are cut from a pattern using shears. The metal is held in a **vice**.

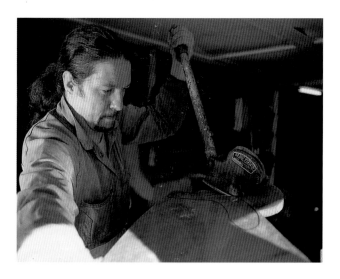

Step 2

The sharp edges are smoothed. This process is called deburring.

Step 3

The pieces are shaped.

CHALLENGE 1

Rewrite this sentence and change the punctuation to give the poor soldier some dignity!

'In came the soldier on his face, a fierce look on his feet, his shoes on his back, his armour shouting his war cry.'

The answer is on page 30.

Step 4

The pieces are buffed to take out any hammer marks.

Step 6

The pauldrons are fitted to the knight's shoulder.

Step 5

The pieces are assembled and joined together.

▼ The knight in his armour

Q Why is it dark in a suit of armour?

The answer is on page 30.

Aprons

An apron is a shield for your clothes. It protects the wearer's clothes from getting dirty. It can also protect the wearer by acting as another layer of clothes. This could be important when cooking, as hot food can splash out of a pan.

In restaurants, the chef usually wears a double-breasted jacket. This means the jacket has two fronts. If one front gets dirty while cooking, the chef switches fronts to look clean again!

► An apron decorated with fish and sea creatures

An embroidered black silk apron
▼ from around 1880

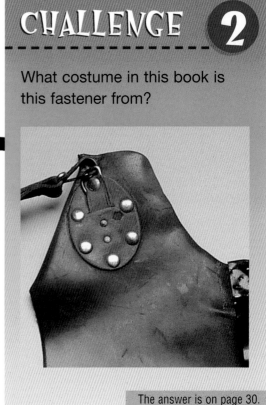

CHALLENGE 2

What costume in this book is this fastener from?

The answer is on page 30.

Mining clothes

Miners who go below ground to dig and extract minerals face many dangers. The mine can collapse and bury them, it can be very cold and damp, it is dark, and the air may not be suitable to breathe. Miners need protection from these dangers.

► This is a Davy lamp, a type of safety lamp developed for miners in England in the early 1800s by Humphrey Davy. The oil lamps were designed so that their flame would not ignite flammable gases or coal dust in the mine.

Before the 1880s, coal miners would take a canary in a cage down the mine shaft with them. If the canary became sick, the miners would leave the area. In the 1880s, miners would carry a lamp with a burning flame. The miner would watch the colour of the flame to see if the air was good or bad.

Nowadays, miners have their own oxygen and a torch as part of their work clothes.

◄ For protection, this miner is wearing a pair of overalls (with reflective stripes), a jacket, rubber boots with steel caps, a helmet, and a belt with accessories including a breathing mask, gas detector, knife and Davy safety lamp.

Sportswear

In ancient times, people wore protective clothing to play war games such as wrestling, fencing and archery. Today, many athletes still wear clothes or equipment to protect themselves. Depending on the sport, they can wear:

- helmets
- shin guards
- mouth guards
- gloves
- bandages
- special shoes
- padding
- shoulder guards.

Their clothing is like armour. It is designed for comfort, speed and protection.

▲ In American football, tackling is very common. Players wear padded clothes and face masks for protection.

◄ Helmets provide protection from head injury. Most deaths among cyclists are from head injuries. Bicycle helmets protect you.

Lisa Keightly, sportswoman

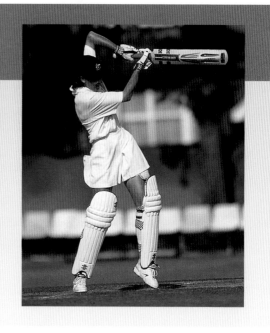

'My name is Lisa Keightly and I am a member of the Australian Women's Cricket Team. One of the highlights of my career was being the first lady to score a century at Lord's [in England]. I would not have been able to achieve this if it wasn't for my protective gear from Gray Nicholls. The protective gear includes cricket pads, thigh guard and batting gloves.'

May 1999

Driving clothes

Special clothes can be worn for driving, especially for motor racing. Jack Brabham won the World Drivers' Championship three times. In 1966, he drove the Repco Brabham, which he designed himself, and won the Championship. Motor racing can be very dangerous. In Jack Brabham's day, his car did not even have a driver harness.

Protection for drivers has improved. For example, in 1980, world champion Alan Jones wore a coverall that gave 50 seconds of fire protection. Strong handles sewn on the shoulders meant that he could be pulled out of his car in an emergency.

▼ Jack Brabham driving in his racing car. He wore an open-faced helmet and a woollen vest.

▶ The first cars did not have a roof and the roads were just dirt tracks. Women wore special clothes, including head scarves, glasses and dustcoats, for protection against the dust, wind and cold.

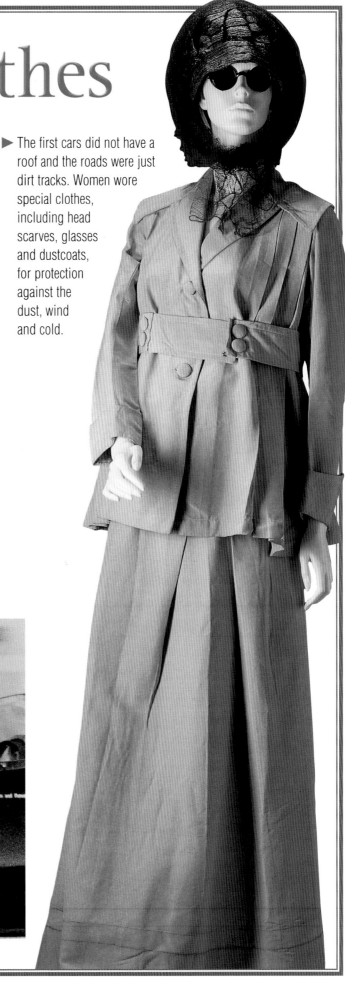

Raincoats

For centuries, people used animal fur to keep warm and dry. Inuit from the Arctic circle wore raincoats made from the intestines of a walrus. In the 1600s, **linseed oil** was added to cotton, or tar to canvas, to make the material waterproof.

- Outer Fabric
- GORE-TEX® Membrane
- Inner Lining
- GORE-SEAM® Tape

▲ How a Gore-Tex® raincoat is constructed.

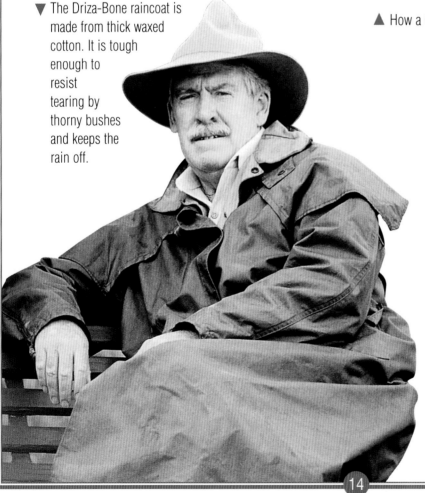

▼ The Driza-Bone raincoat is made from thick waxed cotton. It is tough enough to resist tearing by thorny bushes and keeps the rain off.

Some fabrics that keep water out can trap sweat in. Worn over a long time, some raincoats can make you feel very damp and cold. In the 1970s, a **membrane** was made that had tiny holes in it – too small for rainwater to pass through but big enough to let sweat out. The membrane can be stuck to fabric such as Gore-Tex®. The company that makes Gore-Tex® says this material is 'waterproof, windproof and breathable'.

Diving suits

To stay under water for long periods, people need air and protection from the cold. Auguste Siebe made the first diving suit in 1837. It was a rubberized canvas suit with a helmet clamped onto it and big heavy boots. The air came through a tube from a machine on the land or in a boat.

The first self-contained underwater breathing apparatus (SCUBA) was developed during World War II. Divers no longer needed an airtube to link them to a boat. They had the air on their backs.

▲ A rubberized canvas suit used for gathering pearl shells from the Pacific Ocean around 1885

Computing under water

WetPC™ is a wearable computer worn with a SCUBA for underwater use. It allows a diver to gather and enter data onto a computer under water. To use the computer, the diver presses buttons on their chest or a hand-held key pad. The display is in front of the face mask.

◀ A WetPC™ made by the Australian Institute of Marine Science, 1998

Swimwear

Swimwear can protect people from the water and sun. In the past, swimwear protected people's modesty as well. The size of swimwear has changed over the years. First, it covered a lot of the body, then it got smaller and smaller as people were less embarrassed about showing their body, and now it is getting bigger again to protect the skin from the sun. The material swimwear is made from has also changed a lot. When your great-grandparents were children, their swimming costumes were probably made of wool or thick cotton. Today, swimwear is often made from thin and stretchy **lycra**.

◀ Bathing caps protect
▼ the hair from the sun and pool chemicals and keep the hair dry.

▲ A two-piece swimming costume and matching shirt designed by Nicole Zimmermann, Australia, 1996. For full sun protection, the model should wear both sunscreen and a hat.

Annette Kellerman was a swimmer, water ballerina and film actress who lived between 1886 and 1975. She did things that women did not do in those days. She also created her own style of clothing including swimwear.

▼ In 1907, Annette Kellerman was arrested on a beach in the United States for wearing a one-piece swimsuit that showed her legs. It was too daring! She argued in court that the swimsuit she was wearing would be safer than other swimsuits fashionable at the time.

Meet
Dawn Henderson,
swimwear factory supervisor

▲ Dawn Henderson

How long have you worked at Speedo?

I have been here for 43 years. I was 15 years old when I started at Speedo as the junior girl in the factory. In those days, there were about 30 women in the factory and one man. He was the mechanic. My first job was cutting elastic for men's underwear and all swimwear.

What is your job now?

I am senior supervisor of the whole machinery floor. There are 64 women on this floor and one man.

Is it the same man?

No! But he is the mechanic. There is also a cutting area and warehouse.

Tell me about your work day.

I start at 7.30 a.m. with a chat to the Production Manager. I also talk to the girls that get work ready to go onto the machines. During the day I talk to the three work supervisors. I might visit the small factories that do work for us when we are very busy. I do administrative work to take care of everyone's leave and pay.

What is your favourite part of the job?

It's just a job. I grew up in a time when you had to have a job and you expected to work. This is a pleasant place to work, with good people to work with, so I've stayed with it.

▶ Some of the steps involved in
▼ making Speedo swimwear.

Do you feel very proud when you see Speedo costumes in the Olympic Games?

I look for our costumes in the race. I do feel very proud of our work.

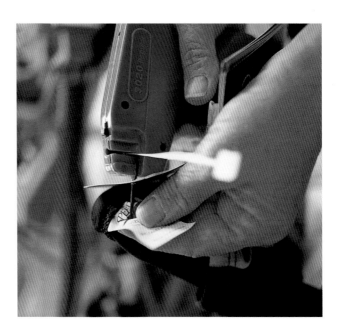

Finished swimsuits like these have been worn by swimmers in Olympic
▶ Games.

Women's swimwear timeline, 1900–50

Bathing suit made from mohair, with bloomers and stockings

Annette Kellerman's new style of swimsuit, made from knitted cotton

1900 ——— **1905** ——— **1910**

One-piece costume or maillot, made from knitted wool

Ballerina suit made from rayon, over trunks

1935 ——— **1940**

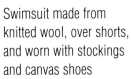

Swimsuit made from knitted wool, over shorts, and worn with stockings and canvas shoes

Swimsuit made from knitted wool, over shorts

1915 — **1920** — **1925** — **1930**

Bikini made from cotton or linen

Bloomer suit made from elastic jersey

1945 — **1950**

Fire-fighting suits

Fires can burn, choke, crush and blind people. Fire-fighters need to wear protective clothing and equipment and be fit. Fire-fighters once wore **asbestos** suits until people found out that breathing in asbestos fibres caused cancer.

The costume for fighting house fires or bushfires today is a special helmet, boots, gloves and coat worn over trousers or overalls.

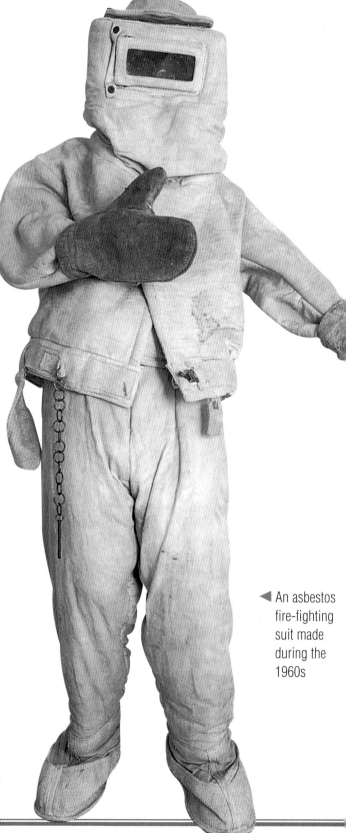

► A fire-fighter in protective clothing

◄ An asbestos fire-fighting suit made during the 1960s

Radiation

Radio, radar, infra-red and X-rays are all forms of electromagnetic radiation. This radiation moves in waves that we cannot see. Some electromagnetic radiation, such as hospital X-rays, burns the body if it is exposed for too long or very often. Electromagnetic radiation waves cannot pass through lead. Lead and rubber aprons protect staff who use X-ray equipment daily.

► This suit is made of PVC with rubber gloves and boots attached. The fire-fighter is enclosed in the suit with their own supply of air. This suit is used when there is an emergency involving hazardous chemicals.

Fire alert!

Remember always to wear pyjamas or nighties that say 'Low flammability'. This means the fabric is slow to burn. Pyjamas and nighties that say 'Keep away from fire' will easily burn, and if the nightwear is loose fitting, it may swing towards a fire or heater.

▲ This lead-lined rubber apron with leather straps and metal buckles is worn by X-ray operators.

Ultraviolet radiation

Ultraviolet radiation (UVR) from the sun damages human skin. Ultraviolet radiation levels can be high even on a cool, cloudy day. They are lower in winter than summer, but still present. Ultraviolet radiation is reflected from snow, water, sand, white walls, light–coloured concrete and even a little from grass and soil.

▼ Wide-brimmed hats help protect the back of your head, your face and your ears from ultraviolet radiation.

▲ This shirt has a collar to protect your neck and sleeves to protect your shoulders from the sun.

The more skin you cover with clothing, the more protected you will be from ultraviolet radiation. The style of clothing, including the weave and colour of the fabric, is important in giving you the maximum sun protection factor (SPF). An SPF of 15+ means that the garment will give you at least 15 times the protection than your skin would have if you did not have the garment on.

▲ Some sunglasses protect your eyes from ultraviolet radiation.

Make a *camera obscura*

It is dangerous to look directly at the sun. However, a *camera obscura* is a safe way of observing the sun.

What you need:

- a cardboard box and lid
- a piece of white paper
- a pair of scissors
- masking tape
- a pin

Step 1

Take a cardboard box and lid. Cut out one end of the box. Stick a piece of paper over the cut-out end of the box.

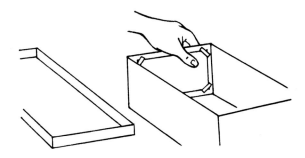

Step 2

Pierce a hole in the opposite end of the box.

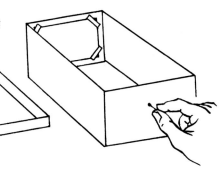

Step 3

Light coming through the hole will project an image of an object outside the box onto the white paper. The image is reversed and upside down.

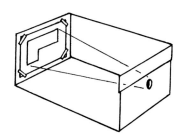

Step 4 (optional)

The image will be very sharp if the box has a larger hole and a small magnifying lens.

Did you know?

Camera is the Latin word for 'chamber' or 'room' and *obscura* means 'dark'.

Flying suits

'Smithy'

Charles Kingsford Smith, or 'Smithy' as he was called, was born in 1897 and died in mysterious circumstances in 1935. Smithy was a World War I fighter pilot, movie stuntman, airline owner, pastoralist and truck driver. Smithy made many epic flights. For example, he was the first to cross the Pacific Ocean by plane – he flew from North America to Australia, and from Australia to North America. He died somewhere over the Bengal Sea, with his co-pilot Tommy Pethybridge, attempting to break the England to Australia record. The two pilots were never found; only the wheel of the plane was found. Charles Kingsford Smith is likely to have been wearing his Sidcot suit – an all-in-one suit made of rubberized linen with a detachable fur collar, and a large pocket on each knee. The suit was done up by zips. It could be worn with a woollen or padded inner lining for warmth. By 1920, the suits were also fireproof.

This flying helmet, worn by Charles Kingsford Smith in 1928, is made of leather and would have kept his head warm.

'Ladybird'

Joan Taubman was an award-winning aerobatic pilot. Nicknamed 'Ladybird', Joan performed fearless stunts in a plane. With no parachute or safety equipment, she must have had nerves of steel!

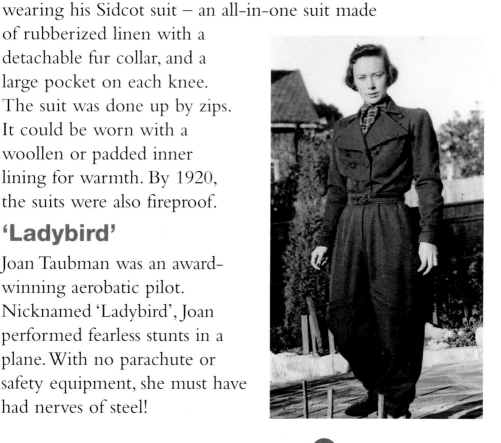

Sidney Cotton designed the Sidcot suit in 1916 to protect pilots from the extreme temperatures in a plane's open cockpit. This Sidcot suit was made for Joan Taubman (left) in 1940.

Masks

Non-woven fabrics

Once, people were less careful about germs because they did not understand that germs spread disease. It took many years of scientists' research and telling people about germs before people changed their habits. Some **non-woven fabric** is made from spun plastic. It can be made in different strengths and thicknesses and has many uses. Non-woven lining in disposable nappies, and in hospital gowns and drapes, is used only once. To stop the spread of infection, the soiled non-woven fabric is thrown away.

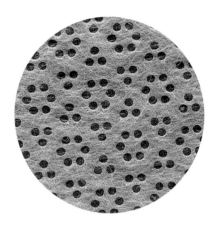

▶ A close-up view of a non-woven fabric.

Masks

During the influenza epidemic of 1919, people wore masks over their faces. This was a worldwide epidemic that killed 20 million people. To try to stop the disease spreading in Australia, passengers on ships from England, South Africa and New Zealand were not allowed to go ashore until a doctor saw them. The government stopped sporting matches where many people came together to watch them. Churches were closed. People wore masks when outside and around other people.

▼ People wearing masks in Sydney during the 1919 influenza epidemic.

Space suits

Space flight meant people had to think about human survival needs very carefully. For astronauts and cosmonauts to survive, they have to have all the things that kept them alive on Earth. They need the right pressure and amount of air to breathe, food, water, temperature and methods of waste disposal. Astronauts have to take their Earth world with them when they go into space.

▶ This is a Russian space suit called a sokol. *Sokol* is the Russian word for 'falcon'. The suit is worn by cosmonauts during take-off and landing in a spacecraft. The suit maintains air pressure around the cosmonaut even if there is a problem with the spacecraft. In 1971, the crew of *Soyuz 11* space mission died because they were not wearing these suits. A small valve in the spacecraft was not working and the air leaked away. Sokol suits have been worn ever since.

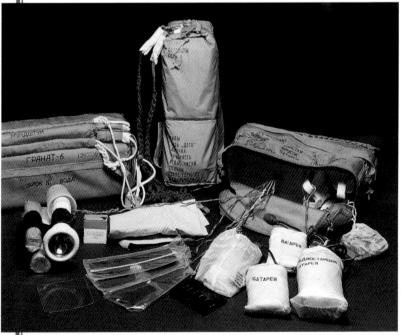

◀ This is the survival kit supplied to the Russian cosmonauts in case their *Soyuz* spacecraft lands off-course. It includes emergency rations and water, medical supplies, tools and a radio. It also has special clothes for different emergency situations. A hydrosuit will inflate to help the cosmonauts float if they land in the water. A cold-weather suit protects the cosmonauts from temperatures as low as −10 degrees.

What they were wearing then

In 1969, Neil Armstrong and Edwin 'Buzz' Aldrin were the first people to walk on the moon. They wore special spacesuits called EMUs (Extra-vehicular Mobility Units). These suits had 23 layers of material to protect the astronauts from the extreme temperatures and lack of air on the moon. The outer layer was a tough material called 'Beta cloth' that was made of **teflon**-coated fabric. It protected the astronauts from the tiny meteorite particles that could tear their suits. Their gloves had fingertips made of **silicone** rubber, so that they could feel what they were doing. The helmets had a special gold-coated screen to protect the astronauts' eyes from the harsh sunlight. The spacesuits' backpack had a life-support system that enabled the astronauts to breathe. Under their spacesuits, Neil and Buzz wore special underwear covered in thin water tubes to help keep them cool.

Safety first

Most costume is, or once was, made to protect. Even jewellery such as pins and brooches, which seem to have little practical or protective function, were first made to hold cloaks together to keep the wearer warm. To survive, our bodies need to be covered, especially when we go to extreme places such as under the sea or out into space. This book has looked at costumes that say 'protection' when you look at them. The costumes are working even if the wearer is playing.

▶ Shoes are an important piece of protective costume. This thick leather boot looks tough and strong. Made around 1790, it was worn by a horse-rider at the front of a team of horses drawing a carriage. The boot protected the rider's leg from being crushed between the lead horses, and from sticks and stones flung up from the road.

Answers

Page 8
'In came the soldier, on his face a fierce look, on his feet his shoes, on his back his armour, shouting his war cry.'

Page 9
Because of the (k)night inside.

Page 10
The fastener is from the lead apron on page 23.

Glossary

armour   the metal or leather covering that warriors use to protect themselves in battle

asbestos   a grey substance mined from the ground and once used to make fireproof materials or fabric

exoskeleton   an external protective covering, for example, the shell of a crab

lacquer   a clear coating put on something to protect it, or make it shiny

linseed oil   the oil from the seed of the flax plant

lycra   a synthetic knitted fabric that can stretch

membrane   a thin sheet of material that allows fluids, like water, to pass through it

non-woven fabric   any fabric made by pressing material together, such as wool into felt, or spun plastic into non-woven fabric

pauldron   a piece of armour that protects the shoulder and upper part of the arm

samurai   Japanese warrior

silicone   a synthetic rubber material that can resist extreme temperatures

teflon   a plastic that is non-stick and resistant to extreme temperatures and radiation

ultraviolet radiation   the rays from the sun that can burn you

vice   a tool that closes around something and holds it tightly in place while you work on it

Index

Photo and objects credits

All objects featured in this publication are from the Powerhouse Museum collection and all photographs are by the Powerhouse Museum, unless otherwise indicated below. Collection objects are reproduced by permission of the designers or makers listed. The museum acknowledges the many generous donations of objects, which form a significant part of its collection.

p3 sunglasses photo, NSW Cancer Council; p4 funkessentials poster by Sara Thorn and Bruce Slorach; p5 raincoat photo, Paddy Pallin Adventure Equipment; nylon sportswear by Kate Sylvester, photo by Karin Catt for *Vogue Australia*; p10 apron by Olive Nock; p11 miner photo, Megan Hicks; p12 gridiron photo, National Sport Information Centre, Australian Sports Commission; Lisa Keightly photo, Sport the library; bicycle rider photo, Roads & Traffic Authority of NSW; p13 Jack Brabham photo by Geoffrey Goddard; p14 Gore-tex® layer diagram, W L Gore & Associates (Australia) Pty Ltd; Driza-Bone photo, *Northern Daily Leader*; p15

Wet PC™, photo, Australian Institute of Marine Science; p16 swimsuit by Nicole Zimmermann, Australia; p17 Annette Kellerman photo from Annette Kellerman papers, Mitchell Library, State Library of NSW; p19 swimwear production, Speedo; pp20/21 timeline based on information from R Turner Wilcox, *The Dictionary of Costume*, B T Batsford, London, 1992; pp22/23 fire fighting suit and hazchem suit, NSW Fire Brigade 1999; asbestos suit by Bestobell 1960s; p23 x-ray protective clothing from the RACR-Robert Bennett Collection; p24 hat, T-shirts and sunglasses photos, NSW Cancer Council; p26 Joan Taubman photo, Joan Taubman; p27 influenza masks photo, National Library of Australia; p28 emergency space kit photo, 1999 Sotheby's, Inc; p29 man on the moon photo, NASA; p31 nylon sportswear by Kate Sylvester, photo by Karin Catt for *Vogue Australia*; p32 hat photo, NSW Cancer Council.

Please visit the Powerhouse Museum at **www.phm.gov.au**